Jump Start Your Career
in Technology & IT
in about 100 Pages

Table of Contents

Let's Start !

Chapter 1 Introduction to Node.js

What is Node.js?

We can obtain information about Node.js at www.nodejs.org. According to the site, "Node.js is a platform built on Chrome's JavaScript runtime for easily building fast, scalable network applications. Node.js uses an event-driven, non-blocking I/O model that makes it lightweight and efficient, perfect for data-intensive real-time applications that run across distributed devices." I suggest you also read the "What is Node.js" thread for a more in-depth Node.js definition.

Node.js provides the complete solution for server-side applications, such as web platforms. It can communicate with other systems, like database, LDAP, and any legacy application. There are many scenarios we can implement for Node.js.

Installation

Node.js can run on Windows, Linux, and Mac. It provides 32-bit and 64-bit platforms. To install Node.js for Ubuntu Linux, use the console and write the following script:

```
sudo apt-get install python-software-properties
sudo add-apt-repository ppa:chris-lea/node.js
sudo apt-get update
sudo apt-get install nodejs npm
```

For complete instructions on how to install Node.js for another Linux platform, visit: https://github.com/joyent/node/wiki/Installing-Node.js-via-package-manager.

If you are a Windows user, you can install Node.js using the setup file. You can download it from the Node.js website, http://nodejs.org/download/. Download the .MSI file according to your platform. Run it and you will get the setup dialog as follows:

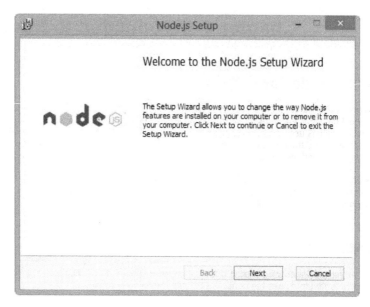

Figure 1: A Node.js Setup dialog

Follow the installation instructions.

A Node.js icon will be created on the Windows menu after installation. If you click this menu, the Node.js console will open.

Figure 2: Node.js console

You can run the Node.js console manually from Windows Command Prompt (CMD). Launch it and type the following:

```
node
```

It will display a response like the Node.js console.

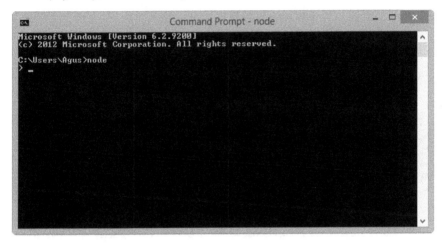

Figure 3: Running Node.js from Command Prompt

Development Tools

You can use any text editor to write Node.js code. If you want to get more development experience, you could use the code editor with rich features such as WebStorm JetBrains, Eclipse, and Visual Studio. Some code editors may provide a debugging feature.

For Visual Studio 2012, you can use a web project template such as ASP.NET Empty Web Site.

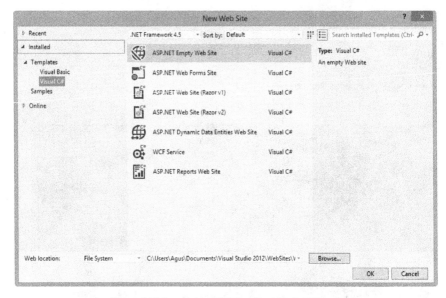

Figure 4: Web project template on Visual Studio 2012

Visual Studio 2012 provides an IntelliSense feature. It can help you to display information about API and syntax.

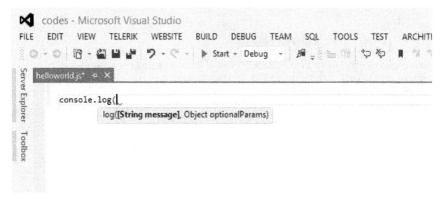

Figure 5: IntelliSense feature on Visual Studio 2012

Hello World

Learning a new programming language usually starts with writing "hello world" code. Now how about Node.js? Let's start writing "hello world" for Node.js.

First, run your code editor and write the following:

```
console.log('Hello world, nodejs');
```

Save this code to a file named **helloworld.js**.

Then open CMD or Terminal (Linux) and execute this file:

```
node helloworld.js
```

Here is the sample output of our "hello world" application:

Figure 6: "Hello world" application for Node.js

Note: console.log() shows data in the console.

Node.js Module

Node.js provides modules to help our development. It is possible to cut development time because you don't need write many lines of code.

There are a lot of Node.js modules that you can use. The list of Node.js modules can be seen here: https://github.com/joyent/node/wiki/Modules.

To install Node.js modules, you need the Node Packaged Modules (npm) package manager. After installing Node.js, you should have the npm package manager. You can check this by typing the script shown in the following table:

```
npm -help
```

Then you will get a response on the console as shown in the following figure:

```
Command Prompt                                           –  □  ×

C:\Users\Agus>npm -help

Usage: npm <command>

where <command> is one of:
    add-user, adduser, apihelp, author, bin, bugs, c, cache,
    completion, config, ddp, dedupe, deprecate, docs, edit,
    explore, faq, find, find-dupes, get, help, help-search,
    home, i, info, init, install, la, link, list, ll, ln, login,
    ls, outdated, owner, pack, prefix, prune, publish, r, rb,
    rebuild, remove, restart, rm, root, run-script, s, se,
    search, set, show, shrinkwrap, star, start, stop, submodule,
    tag, test, tst, un, uninstall, unlink, unpublish, unstar,
    up, update, version, view, whoami

npm <cmd> -h        quick help on <cmd>
npm -l              display full usage info
npm faq             commonly asked questions
npm help <term>     search for help on <term>
npm help npm        involved overview

Specify configs in the ini-formatted file:
    C:\Users\Agus\.npmrc
or on the command line via: npm <command> --key value
Config info can be viewed via: npm help config

npm@1.1.62 C:\Program Files\nodejs\node_modules\npm

C:\Users\Agus>
```

Figure 7: Calling the npm package manager

Let's start to use a Node.js module, for instance, to add color to our console text. The module is cli-color, https://github.com/medikoo/cli-color.

First, install the cli-color module:

```
npm install cli-color
```

 Note: To install a Node.js module, your computer must be able to access an internet network. Some modules may require administrator level privileges for installation.

The output of installation is shown in Figure 8.

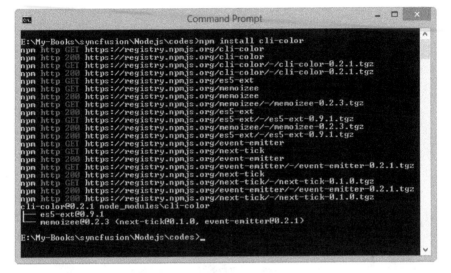

Figure 8: cli-color module installation

How do we use this module?

We need call the Node.js module in our code by calling require with the module name.

```
var clc = require('cli-color');
```

Therefore, if we want to color text, we can call xxx.blue for blue text and xxx.green for green text. xxx is a cli-color object.

```
console.log(clc.blue('"Hello node.js" in blue'));
console.log(clc.red('"Hello node.js" in red'));
console.log(clc.green('"Hello node.js" in green'));
```

The sample of program output can be seen in Figure 9.

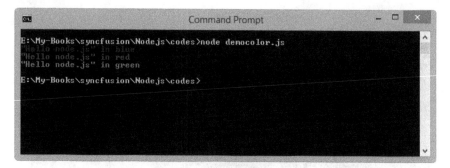

Figure 9: Program output for Node.js application with cli-color module.

Updating Node.js Version

How do you know the version of Node.js you are working with?

You can use a Node.js command to get the information on your Node.js version. Write this script:

```
node -v
```

This is the output of Node.js script:

Figure 10: Getting the current Node.js version

Node.js doesn't automatically update the existing runtime. You should check and update the Node.js version manually. Download the setup file from the Node.js website and then install it on your computer.

The setup installation will check the installed Node.js. If it was found, it will update the current version of Node.js. Check your Node.js version again after installation is complete.

Chapter 2 Basic Node.js Programming

This chapter will describe some basic Node.js programming. Node.js uses the JavaScript language to write code. If you have experienced programming in JavaScript, you will find it easier to write Node.js code.

Defining Variables

Node.js has a rule to define variables. Basically, we can declare a variable in Node.js to the following:

```
var variable_name;
```

variable_name is your variable name. The following illustrates an example of declaring a Node.js variable:

```
var firstName;
var lastName;
var age;
```

We can assign values to our variables:

```
firstName = "Alexander";
lastName = "King"
age = 10;
```

We also can assign values directly when declaring variables:

```
var firstName = "Alexander";
var lastName = "King";
var age = 10;
```

In Node.js or JavaScript, we can declare a variable without defining a specific data type. We can use var for the data type. If we assign a string value then our variable will become a string data type.

```
var city = "Berlin";
var id = 5;
```

In general, we can declare a variable name with any name, but you must avoid usage of JavaScript keywords. Here is the list of keywords to avoid:

- break
- case
- catch
- continue
- debugger
- default
- delete
- do
- else
- finally
- for

- new
- package
- private
- protected
- public
- function
- if
- implements
- in
- instanceof
- interface

- return
- static
- switch
- this
- throw
- try
- typeof
- var
- void
- while
- with

Comment

You may explain how to work on your code as a note or comment. In Node.js, we can write a note or a comment using // and /* */ syntax. The following is a sample code:

```
// bank account
var account;

/* parameters*/
var p1, p2, p3, p4;
```

Arithmetic Operations

Node.js supports four basic arithmetic operations: addition, subtraction, multiplication, and division.

Table 1: Basic arithmetic operations in Node.js

Node.js Code	Note
+	Addition
-	Subtraction
*	Multiplication
/	Division

The following is the code illustration for basic arithmetic using Node.js.

```
var a, b;
a = 10;
b = 5.4;

// Addition
var c = a + b;
console.log(c);

// Subtraction
var c = a - b;
console.log(c);

// Multiplication
var c = a * b;
console.log(c);

// Division
var c = a / b;
console.log(c);
```

Save this code into a file, for instance **basicarith.js**. If you run this code, you will get the program output shown in Figure 11.

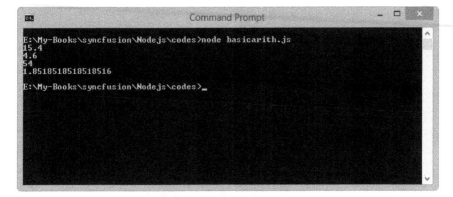

Figure 11: The program output for arithmetic operations

Mathematical Functions

Node.js provides a math library based on the JavaScript library. Here is the list of mathematical functions:

- Math.abs(a), the absolute value of a

- Math.acos(a), arc cosine of a

- Math.asin(a), arc sine of a

- Math.atan(a), arc tangent of a

- Math.atan2(a,b), arc tangent of a/b

- Math.ceil(a), integer closest to a and not less than a

- Math.cos(a), cosine of a

- Math.exp(a), exponent of a (Math.E to the power a)

- Math.floor(a), integer closest to a, not greater than a

- Math.log(a), log of a base e

- Math.max(a,b), the maximum of a and b

- Math.min(a,b), the minimum of a and b

- Math.pow(a,b), a to the power b

- Math.random(), pseudorandom number 0 to 1 (see examples)

- Math.round(a), integer closest to a (see rounding examples)

- Math.sin(a), sine of a

- Math.sqrt(a), square root of a

- Math.tan(a), tangent of a

To get an understanding of the math library usage, write this script:

```
var a, b;
a = 2;
b = 3.5;

console.log(Math.sin(a));
console.log(Math.cos(b));
console.log(Math.max(a, b));
console.log(Math.sqrt(a * b));
```

Save this script into a file and run it in the console using Node.js.

You can see the output of our script in Figure 12.

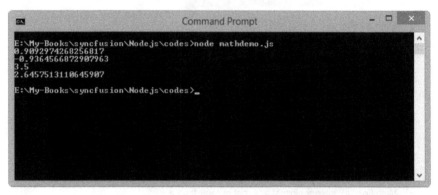

Figure 12: The program output for basic math operations

Comparison Operators

You may determine equality or difference among variables or values. For instance, you have two values 10 and 20, and you want to compare these values. Node.js adopts C language for comparison operator syntax. The following is the list of comparison operators.

Table 2: Comparison operators in Node.js

Node.js Comparison	Note
==	Equal to
!=	Not equal
>	Greater than
<	Less than
>=	Greater than or equal to
<=	Less than or equal to

Let's write script for comparison usage for Node.js.

```
var a, b;
a = 5;
b = 8;

console.log(a > b);
console.log(a < b);
console.log(a >= b);
console.log(a <= b);
console.log(a != b);
console.log(a == b);
```

You can see the program output in Figure 13.

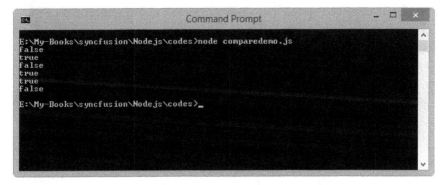

Figure 13: The program output for comparison operator usage

Logical Operators

Node.js supports logical operation. These logical operators can be used to determine the logic between variables or value. You can see in Table 3 how Node.js implements logical operators.

Table 3: Logical operators in Node.js

Logical Operators	Note
&&	And
||	Or
!	Not

Here is the script sample that illustrates logical operation:

```
var a, b;
a = 5;
b = 8;

console.log(a > b && a != b);
console.log(!(a >= b));
console.log(a == b || a > b);
```

Run it using Node.js and you will see the program output shown in Figure 14.

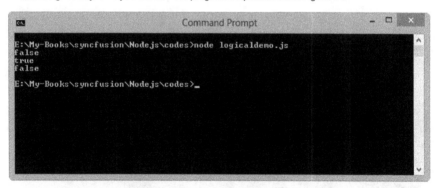

Figure 14: The program output for logical operation in Node.js

Increment and Decrement

Imagine you have a value and you want this value to be incremented by 1. In general, you may implement the following script:

```
var a = 5;
a = a + 1;
```

We can do another solution with ++ syntax. We can rewrite our script to the following:

```
var a = 5;
a++;
```

We also can apply decrement in our value by using - syntax:

```
var b = 8;
b++;
```

Decision

A computer can execute instructions that are clear and precise. The computer will always do exactly what you say. That's both good and bad news. The problem is that the computer follows instructions even if they are absurd; it has no judgment with which to question anything.

Our code can decide what the computer will do. It's a decision. We can implement a decision in our program behavior like "if A is true, then do B". In Node.js, we have two options to implement a decision program:

- if..then
- switch..case

if... then

The following is syntax for decision in Node.js:

```
if(condition){
    do_something_a;
}else {
    do_something_b;
}
```

If the condition is true, then it will execute do_something_a.

Let's write a script to implement a decision program in Node.js.

```
var a, b;
a = 5;
b = 8;

if (a > b || a - b < a) {
    console.log('conditional-->a>b || a-b<a');
} else {
    console.log('..another');
}
```

Run it using Node.js. Figure 15 is a sample output.

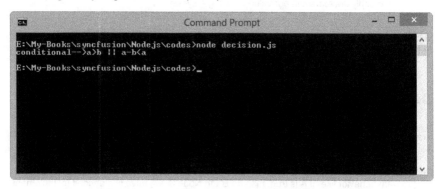

Figure 15: Sample output for decision program by using if..then

Change a and b values, then run it again.

For alternative if-conditional usage, we can use the following form:

```
var a = 8, b = 3;
console.log(a > b ? false : true);
console.log(a==b ? 'a==b' : 'a is not equal to b');
```

switch... case

We can use switch...case syntax to implement decision behavior in our program. The following is a syntax model for switch..case.

```
switch (option) {
    case option1:
        // do option1 job
        break;
    case option2:
        // do option2 job
        break;
}
```

The **option** value can be a string or numeric data type.

For sample illustration, write this script:

```
var color = 'green';

switch (color) {
    case 'black':
        console.log('black');
        break;
    case 'green':
        console.log('green');
        break;
    case 'white':
        console.log('white');
        break;
}
```

Run it and you will get an output response, shown in Figure 16.

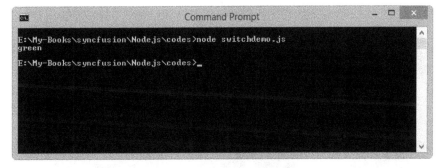

Figure 16: Program output for switch case

You may change the option value in numeric data type. If you change it, you must change the options in case syntax.

Iterations

One of the most powerful concepts in any programming language is that of iterations. It's one of the things that enable a program to do far more than perform a simple calculation and quit. In this section, you'll see how a few lines of Node.js can set up an operation to be performed potentially thousands of times.

Node.js uses **for** and **while** for iteration operation. We will evaluate these syntaxes.

For

The for statement provides this mechanism, letting you specify the **initializer**, **condition**, and **increment/decrement** in one compact line. The following is node.js syntax of the iteration for.

```
for (initialize; condition; increment / decrement) {
    // do something
}
```

Let's start to write this script.

```
for (var counter = 0; counter < 10; counter++) {
    console.log(counter);
}
```

We can see our initial value is 0. This will run until the condition value is not met. Each iteration will do a value addition. Figure 17 is an example of the output from running program.

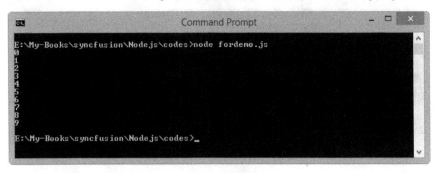

Figure 17: Program output for for-iteration operation

While

Node.js has the simple form of while syntax. The following is a form you can use.

```
while (condition) {
    // do something
}
```

while evaluates the **condition** and executes the statement if that **condition** is true. Then it repeats that operation until the condition evaluates as false.

Now let's use node.js code to implement the while syntax described.

```
var num = 0;

while (num < 10) {
    console.log(num);
    num++;
}
```

The program prints the output, shown in Figure 18.

Figure 18: Program output for while usage

Chapter 3 Array

Node.js provides an Array object for collection manipulation. In general, a Node.js Array object has the same behavior with a JavaScript Array object. In this section, we are going to manipulate an Array object in Node.js

Creating an Array Object

There are three ways to create an Array object. The first is simply by typing the array object.

```
var array = [];
```

Option two is to create an Array object by instantiating the Array object.

```
var array = new Array();
```

The last option is to create an Array object by inserting collection data.

```
var array = [3,5,12,8,7];
```

Inserting Data

After creating an Array object, we can insert data. Use [ ] with index if you want to assign the value.

```
array[0] = 3;
array[1] = 5;
array[2] = 12;
array[3] = 8;
array[4] = 7;
```

You can also use the push( ) function to insert data.

```
array.push(10);
array.push(18);
```

Accessing Data

To access array data, you can use [] with data index parameter.

```
// show data
console.log(array);
for(var i=0;i<array.length;i++){
    console.log(array[i]);
}
```

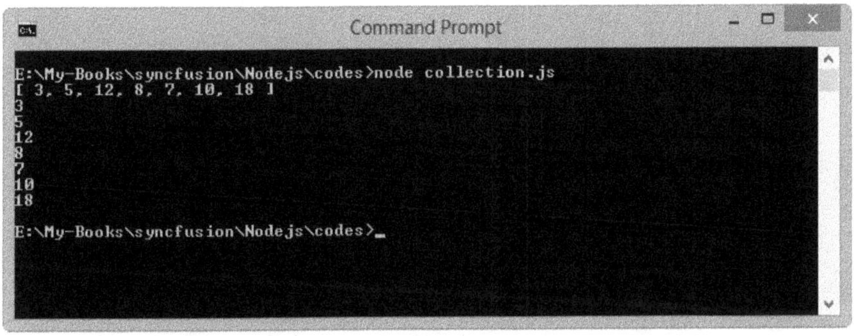
Command Prompt
E:\My-Books\syncfusion\Nodejs\codes>node collection.js
[3, 5, 12, 8, 7, 10, 18]
3
5
12
8
7
10
18
E:\My-Books\syncfusion\Nodejs\codes>

Figure 19: Showing array data

Updating Data

To update an item of array data, you can use [] with data index and thus assign a new value.

```
// edit
array[2] = -2;
array[3] = 5;
console.log(array);
```

Removing Data

You can use the pop() function to remove data from the Array. If you want to remove data by specific index then you can use the `splice()`function.

The following is a sample script for removing data:

```
// remove data
array.pop();
array.pop();

// remove data by index
var index = 1;
array.splice(index,1);
console.log(array);
```

Chapter 4 JSON

JSON (JavaScript Object Notation) is a lightweight data-interchange format. Node.js supports JSON objects for data communication. For further information about JSON, you can visit the official JSON website, http://www.json.org .

Creating a JSON Object

A JSON object in Node.js uses { } syntax to declare the JSON data type. For instance, we have a JSON object called **customer**. This object has the attributes **name**, **email**, **age** and **registeredDate**. The following is an illustration code to declare the **customer** variable as JSON data.

```
var customer = {
    name: 'Michael Z',
    email: 'michael@email.com',
    age: 35,
    registeredDate: new Date()
}
```

You can see that the JSON object consists of a list of the key-value pairs.

You will probably define a nested JSON object. The following is a sample script:

```
var customer = {
    name: 'Michael Z',
    email: 'michael@email.com',
    age: 35,
    registeredDate: new Date(),
    address: {
        city: 'Berlin',
        country: 'Berlin'
    }
}
```

Displaying Data

After you have created the JSON object, you use console.log() to see your object.

```
console.log(customer);
```

It will show a native JSON object in the console.

Figure 20 shows a sample of the JSON object.

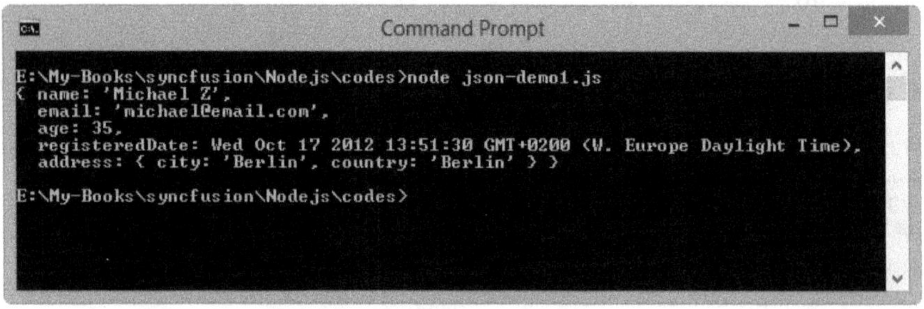

Figure 20: Display JSON object

Accessing Data

As you know, console.log() can display all JSON attributes. If you want to get a specific attribute of a JSON object, then you can call the attribute name directly.

For instance, we can use the **customer** object and display **name**, **email**, **age**, and **registeredDate**. Write this script:

```
console.log('Name:' + customer.name);
console.log('Email:' + customer.email);
console.log('Age:' + customer.age);
console.log('Registered Date:' + customer.registeredDate);
```

Figure 21: Display a specific attribute of JSON object

If you call an unknown attribute of a JSON object, you will get an **undefined** value. For instance, if you call the country attribute in the following script:

```
console.log('Name:' + customer.name);
console.log('Email:' + customer.email);
console.log('Age:' + customer.age);
console.log('Registered Date:' + customer.registeredDate);

console.log('Country:' + customer.country);
```

You will get the response shown in Figure 22.

Figure 22: Accessing an unknown attribute of a JSON object

You may have questioned how we know our JSON object attributes. You can use an iteration operation to get JSON object attributes.

Let's write our script as follows:

```
var myjson = {
    id: 2,
    name: 'jackson',
    email: 'jackson@email.com'
};

for(var att in myjson){
    console.log(att);
}
```

You can see a list of object attributes in Figure 23.

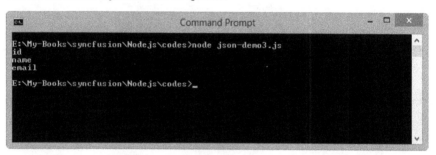

Figure 23: Displaying JSON object attribute names

Imagine you want to check if the attribute name exists in our JSON object. To do this, you can use the hasOwnProperty() function.

The following is a sample script.

```
var myjson = {
    id: 2,
    name: 'jackson',
    email: 'jackson@email.com'
};

// check attribute
console.log(myjson.hasOwnProperty('id'));
console.log(myjson.hasOwnProperty('name'));
console.log(myjson.hasOwnProperty('email'));
console.log(myjson.hasOwnProperty('home'));
```

If you run it, you will get the program output shown in Figure 24.

Figure 24: Checking the existence of JSON object attribute

Editing Data

Editing JSON data can be performed by assigning new values to the object's attribute. For instance, we want to edit the **customer** JSON object. You can see a sample in the following code table:

```
customer.email = 'michael2012@email.com';
customer.age = 33;
console.log(customer);
```

Another solution is to use [ ] with the attribute name to edit value data.

```
var myjson = {
    id: 2,
    name: 'jackson',
    email: 'jackson@email.com'
};

console.log(myjson);

myjson['country'] = 'germany';
console.log(myjson);
```

A sample of the program output is shown in Figure 23.

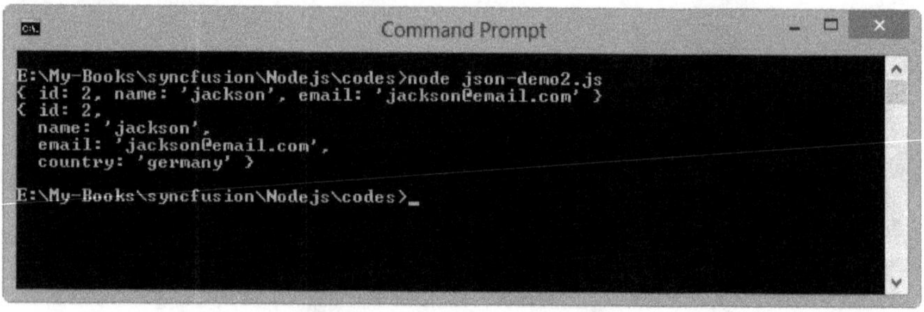

Figure 25: Display edited JSON data

JSON Array

We have already learned Node.js collection. Now we want to combine JSON and collection. This means we create a collection of JSON objects.

To illustrate the JSON array, we create a **productTransaction** object. It consists of transaction information and a list of purchased products.

```
var now = new Date();
var productTransaction = {
    id : 2,
    user: 'agusk',
    transactionDate: now,
    details:[
        {
            code: 'p01',
            name: 'ipad 3',
            price: 600
        },
        {
            code: 'p02',
            name: 'galaxy tab',
            price: 500
        },
        {
            code: 'p03',
            name: 'kindle',
            price: 120
        }
    ]
}
```

You can see that the **details** attribute consists of an array object.

If you display it in the console, you will get the JSON object shown in Figure 26.

```
console.log(productTransaction);
```

Figure 26: Display JSON array object

We can get JSON data through its attributes, for instance, id and call
productTransaction.id:

```
console.log('Id:' + productTransaction.id);
console.log('User:' + productTransaction.user);
console.log('Transaction date:' + productTransaction.transactionDate);
console.log('Details:' + productTransaction.details);
```

If you want to access a JSON array, for instance, using the **details** attribute, you can pass the
index parameter to get a single JSON object.

```
for(var i=0;i<productTransaction.details.length;i++){
    console.log('Code:' + productTransaction.details[i].code);
    console.log('Name:' + productTransaction.details[i].name);
    console.log('Price:' + productTransaction.details[i].price);
}
```

The sample of program output from this script can be seen in Figure 27.

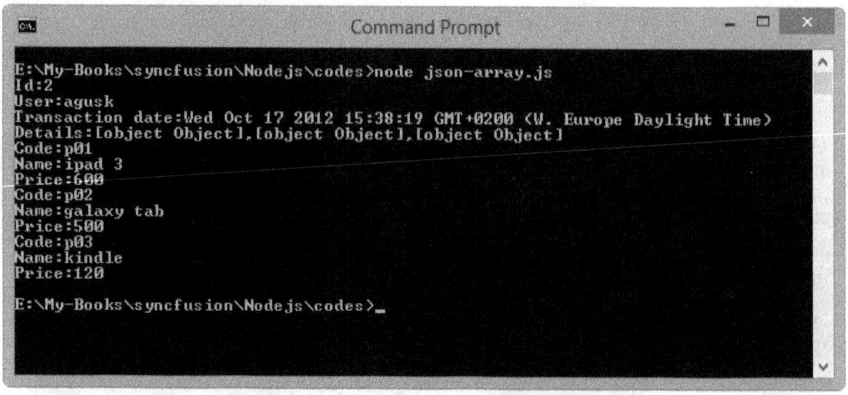

Figure 27: Accessing JSON array object

You can see when we call this script:

```
console.log('Details:' + productTransaction.details);
```

You get the array object as shown in the following code sample:

```
Details:[object Object],[object Object],[object Object]
```

You should call each attribute to get the attribute value.

How do we edit our JSON array object?

You can edit JSON through its attributes. For a JSON array, you must pass the index parameter on A collection attribute, for instance, **details**[index].

```
productTransaction.user = 'zahra';
productTransaction.details[0]['price'] = 250;
console.log(productTransaction);
```

In the previous section, we learned how to check if the attribute name exists or not. We can do this for a JSON array, too.

Here is a sample script.

```
console.log(productTransaction['id']== undefined? false:true);
console.log(productTransaction['name']== undefined? false:true);
console.log(productTransaction.details[0]['code']== undefined? false:true);
console.log(productTransaction.details[0]['approved']== undefined?
false:true);
```

You can see **details**[0]. This means we want to use the array object with index 0.

Figure 28: Checking if the attribute name exists or not in a JSON array object

Chapter 5 Functions

This chapter will describe some basic Node.js programming to create a function.

Creating Function

Declaring a function in Node.js is simple. Here is a function style in Node.js:

```
function function_name(par) {
    // code
}
```

function_name is a function name. par is function parameter.

Let's write a function called myfunction.

```
function myfunction(){
    console.log('calling myfunction');

}
```

You could call it by writing the function name with ( ).

```
myfunction();
```

Save it into a file called function1.js. Run it using Node.js:

```
Node function1.js
```

You can see the output of the program in the following image:

Figure 29: Running a simple program calling the function

Function with a Returning Value

You may want to create a function that has a return value. It is easy because you just call return into your function.

We can use `return` `<value>` at the end of our functions.

```
function getCurrentCity(){

    return 'Berlin';
}
```

Now the function has a return value so we need to get a return value when calling the function.

```
var ret = getCurrentCity();
console.log(ret);
```

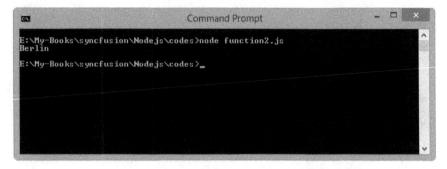

Figure 30: Program output for a function with returning value

Function with Parameters and a Returning Value

You also could create a function with parameters and a returning value. Here is a code illustration:

```
function add(a,b){

    return a+b;
}
```

You can use it in your code as follows:

```
var result = add(10,15);
console.log(result);
```

Figure 31: Program output for a function with parameter and returning a value

Callback Function

A callback function is a function that is called through a function pointer. If you pass the pointer (address) of a function as an argument to another and that pointer is used to call the function it points to, it is said that a callback is made.

How to write a callback function in Node.js?

You can write this code for implementing a callback function:

```
function perform(a,b,callback){
    var c = a*b + a;
    callback(c);
}
```

You can see callback is a function pointer.

Now you can call a callback function in your code.

```
perform(10,5,function(result){
    console.log(result);
})
```

Values 10 and 5 are function parameters. We also pass a function with a parameter result. This parameter is used to get a return value from the callback function.

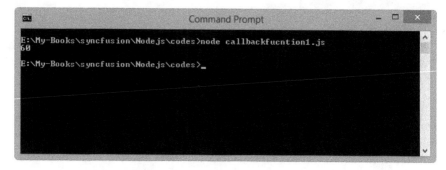

Figure 32: Program output for a callback function

You can define a callback function with many parameters, for example, check this code:

```
function perform(a,b,callback){
    // do processing

    var errorCode = 102;

    callback(errorCode,'Internal server error');
}
```

Then use this callback function in code as follows:

```
perform(10,5,function(errCode,msg){
    if(errCode){
        console.log(msg);
    }
})
```

First check the errCode value. If it has a value, then the code will write the message msg in the console.

This function is very useful when you want to implement a long process. The caller will be notified if the process was done.

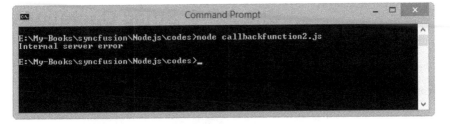

Figure 33: Running a callback function program with a returning value

Chapter 6 String Operations

The string type represents a sequence of zero or more Unicode characters. In Node.js, string type is defined in String. This chapter will describe some basic Node.js programming for string manipulation.

Declaring String Type

You can define a string type object in two forms.

```
var obj1 = new String("hello world");
var obj2 = "hello world";
```

Concatenating String

If you have a list of string data, you can concatenate it into one string.

For instance, you have a list of string data as follows:

```
var str1 = 'hello ';
var str2 = 'world ';
var str3 = 'nodejs';
```

Now you can concatenate all of the data into one variable with a string type. You can use the + operator. Here is a sample code:

```
console.log(str1 + str2 + str3);
```

You can see a sample of program output for this code in the following image:

Figure 34: Program output for concatenating string

String to Numeric

Sometimes you may want to do math operations, but the input data is String type. To convert String type data into numeric, you can use parseInt() for String to Int and parseFloat() for String to Float.

Here is a sample code for string conversion manipulation:

```
console.log('-----parseInt-----');
console.log(parseInt('123'));
console.log(parseInt('123.45'));
console.log(parseInt('-123'));
console.log(parseInt('0.34'));
console.log(parseInt('12abc'));

console.log('-----parseFloat-----');
console.log(parseFloat('123'));
console.log(parseFloat('123.45'));
console.log(parseFloat('-123'));
console.log(parseFloat('0.34'));
console.log(parseFloat('12abc'));
```

If you run it, you will get a console output, shown in Figure 35.

As you see, parseInt() rounds the number. In this example, '123.45' was written 123.45. If string data has non-numeric characters, for instance '12abc', the parseInt() function removes non-numeric characters, so it was written as 123.

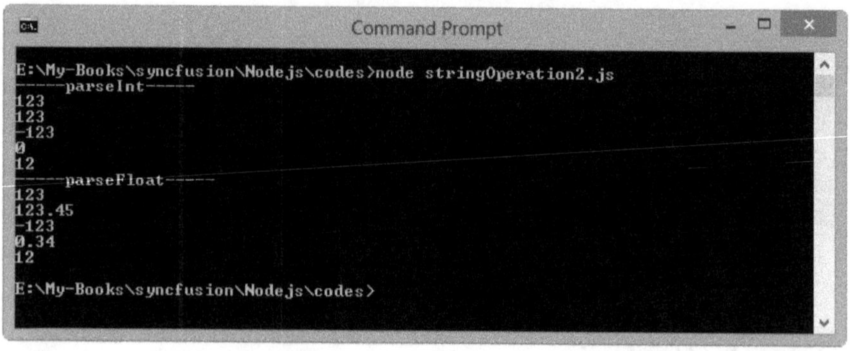

Figure 35: Program output for a string to numeric application

Numeric to String

It is easy to convert numeric data into string type data. You just add ' ' and get string type data automatically.

```
var a = 123;
var b = a + '';
```

Another solution is the toString() method.

```
var num = 405;
var str = num.toString();
```

String Parser

If you have data, for instance, 'Berlin;Amsterdam;London;Jakarta', then you want to parse by using a character as a separator. The simple solution to parsing String uses split() with a parameter delimiter, for instance, ';'. Here is a sample code for this scenario:

```
var data = 'Berlin;Amsterdam;London;Jakarta';
var strs = data.split(';');
for(var index in strs){
    console.log(strs[index]);
}
```

Run this code and you will get a response output, shown in Figure 36.

Figure 36: Parsing data using split()

Check String Data Length

How do you check the length of string data? It's easy. You can call length from the string variable.

```
var str1 = 'hello world, nodejs';
console.log(str1);
console.log('Total string:' + str1.length);
```

The sample of program output is shown in Figure 37.

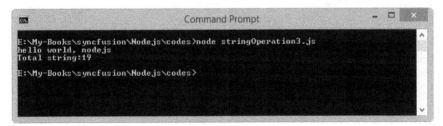

Figure 37: Getting the length of string data

Copy Data

You may copy some characters from String data. To do this, you can use the `substring()` and `substr()` functions. Here is the syntax format:

```
substring(first_index, last_index);
substr(first_index, length);
```

`first_index` is the index where at which extraction starts. The first character is at index 0.

`last_index` is the index at which extraction stops. This is optional. If omitted, it extracts the rest of the string.

`length` is the number of characters to extract. This is optional too. If omitted, it extracts the rest of the string.

The following is the sample code for `substring()` usage:

```
var  str1 = 'hello world, nodejs';

console.log(str1.substring(2,8));
console.log(str1.substring(1,5));
console.log(str1.substring(0,6));
console.log(str1.substring(0,str1.length));
```

Figure 38: Program output for substring() usage

The following is the sample code for `substr()` usage:

```
var str1 = 'hello world, nodejs';

console.log(str1.substr(2,6));
console.log(str1.substr(5,4));
console.log(str1.substr(0,6));
console.log(str1.substr(0,str1.length));
```

```
E:\My-Books\syncfusion\Nodejs\codes>node stringOperation7.js
llo wo
 wor
hello
hello world, nodejs

E:\My-Books\syncfusion\Nodejs\codes>_
```

Figure 39: Program output for substr() usage

Upper and Lower Case Characters

In some situations, you want all string data in uppercase or lowercase characters. This feature is built in the String object. The toUpperCase() function is used to make the whole string uppercase and toLowerCase() is used to make the whole string lowercase.

Here is sample code:

```
var str1 = 'Hello WORLD, nodejs';

console.log(str1.toUpperCase());
console.log(str1.toLowerCase());
```

Run it and you will get the output shown in Figure 40.

Figure 40: Program output for uppercase and lowercase applications

Getting String Index

Each character has an index number that gives its position in the string. We get the index using indexOf() and lastIndexOf(). Here is sample code for getting the index:

```
var  str = 'Hello WORLD, nodejs';

console.log('-----indexOf-----');
console.log(str.indexOf('ello'));
console.log(str.indexOf('nodejs'));
console.log(str.indexOf('e'));

console.log('-----lastIndexOf-----');
console.log(str.lastIndexOf('ello'));
console.log(str.lastIndexOf('nodejs'));
console.log(str.lastIndexOf('e'));
```

Run it. The sample of the program output is shown in Figure 41.

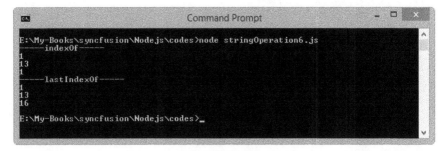

Figure 41: Indexing on String data type

What will happen if you set a value which doesn't exist in string data?

Let's write this code.

```
var  str = 'Hello WORLD, nodejs';
console.log(str.indexOf('C#'));
```

If you run it, you will get the value -1. It means the code didn't find the input in the data. The program output can be shown in Figure 42.

The indexOf() and lastIndexOf() functions apply a case-sensitive method; that is, words can differ in meaning based on use of uppercase and lowercase letters.

Figure 42: Getting value -1 if the program cannot find the characters

Exploring Characters

You may get a character by a specific position index. The charAt() function provides this feature. The first index is 0.

```
var data = 'Berlin;Amsterdam;London;Jakarta';
console.log(data.charAt(0));
console.log(data.charAt(4));
console.log(data.charAt(7));
console.log(data.charAt(10));
```

Run it.

Figure 43: Program output for charAt() function usage

If you have code as follows:

```
var data = 'Berlin;Amsterdam;London;Jakarta';
console.log(data.charAt(100));
```

You will get an empty character, i.e. ''. You can see the sample of program output in Figure 44.

Figure 44: charAt() function generates empty character

Chapter 7 Building Your Own Module

In the previous chapter, we learned about functions. We can create a function and call it in our code. Now, we're going to learn about modules.

Consider you have a function. You want to call this function in many files. The simple solution is to write this function to each *.js file. If you change it, you must change it in all *.js files. For this situation, we need a module. We write a function once in a module. Then, it will be called by attaching this module.

Creating a Simple Module

We can create a simple function and then it will be exported as a module.

Let's write the code:

```
var calculate = function(numA,numB){

    return numA*numB + 10*numB;
}
exports.calculate = calculate;
```

You can see that we can use exports to expose our functions. Save this code into a file, called MyModule.js.

To call this module from our code, we can use require.

```
var myModule = require('./MyModule.js');

var result = myModule.calculate(20,10);
console.log(result);
```

require needs the full path of the module. './' means the module has the same location with the caller. Save this code into a file called testModule.js. Run it:

```
node testModule.js
```

The program output of the application can be seen in Figure 45.

Figure 45: Consuming module in Node.js

You also can create many functions to be exported in the module. Here is sample code:

```
var calculate = function(numA,numB){

    return numA*numB + 10*numB;
}

var add = function(numA,numB){

    return numA + numB;
}
var perform = function(){

    // do something
}

exports.calculate = calculate;
exports.add = add;
exports.perform = perform;
```

Module Class

If you have experience in object-oriented programming, you may implement a class in Node.js. Of course, you can create a class as a module in Node.js.

For instance, we create a class, called Account. First, create a file called Account.js and write this code:

```
// constructor
var Account = module.exports = function(){
    console.log('constructor');
}

// method
Account.prototype.perform = function(){
    console.log('perform');
}

// method
Account.prototype.foo = function(a,b){
    console.log('foo - ' + a + '-' + b);
}
```

We expose our class using module.exports. Then we implement class methods using prototype.

Now we test this class.

Let's write this:

```
var Account = require('./Account.js');
var account = new Account();

account.perform();
```

You can see that we need to instantiate our object by calling new Account().Save this code into a file called testAccount.js. Run it:

```
node testAccount.js
```

The sample of program output can be seen in Figure 46.

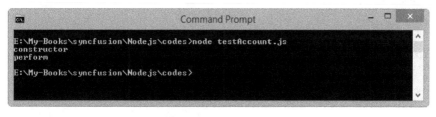

Figure 46: Implementing class in a module

Chapter 8 Error Handling and Logging

Error handling refers to the programming practice of anticipating and coding for error conditions that may arise when your program runs. In this chapter, we're going to learn how to handle errors in Node.js.

Error Handling

We cannot assure our code runs well. Because of this, we should think about how to handle errors. To do so, we can use try..catch syntax. Here is the error handling format in Node.js:

```
try{

    var c = n/b;
    if(c==Infinity)
        throw new Error('this error is caused by invalid operation');

}catch (err){
    console.log(err);
}
```

Let's write this code.

```
var  n = 3;
var b = 0;
try{

    var c = n/b;
    if(c==Infinity)
        throw new Error('this error is caused by invalid operation');

}catch (err){
    console.log(err);
}
```

You can see the n/b operation returns an Infinity value. In this situation, we can throw our error so it will be caught.

If you run this code, you will get the program output shown in Figure 47.

E:\My-Books\syncfusion\Node.js\codes>node error-handling.js
[Error: this error is caused by invalid operation]

E:\My-Books\syncfusion\Node.js\codes>

Figure 47: Catching an error in Node.js

Logging

In the previous section, we used `console.log()` to print an error message in the console. Imagine there are many messages in the console and we want to identify which error message is occurring. The simple solution is to apply font color to the message to identify an error occurring.

Alternatively we can use `log4js-node`. To install this module, write this script:

```
sudo npm install log4js -g
```

For the Windows platform, you should run it under administrator level. You can do it using **RunAs** in the console:

```
npm install log4js -g
```

If you don't install it globally, you can execute as follows:

```
npm install log4js
```

If it is installed successfully, you will get a response output as shown in Figure 48.

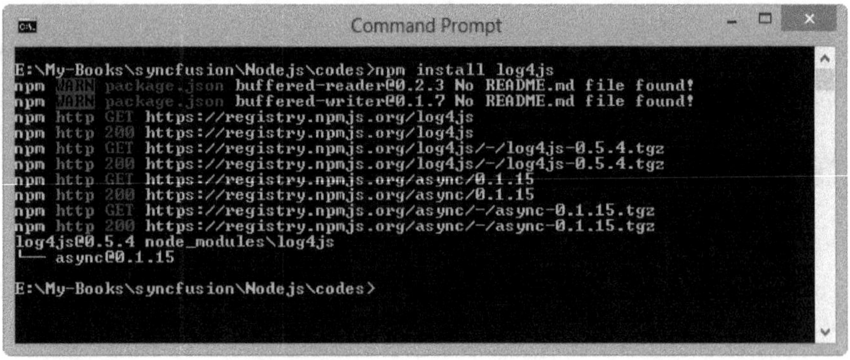

Figure 48: Installing log4js-node

How do we use this module? Let's write the sample code:

```
var log4js = require('log4js');
var logger = log4js.getLogger();

logger.info('Application is running');
logger.warn('Module cannot be loaded');
logger.error('Saved data was error');
logger.fatal('Server could not process');
logger.debug("Some debug messages");
```

Save it into a file called logger-demo.js. Run the file:

```
node logger-demo.js
```

You will see the program output as shown in Figure 49. You can see log4js-node display color text is based on log type.

You could change the display text (**default**) by application category. Just write the category on getLogger( ), for instance, **myapplication**.

```
var log4js = require('log4js');
var logger = log4js.getLogger('myapplication');

logger.info('Application is running');
logger.warn('Module cannot be loaded');
logger.error('Saved data was error');
logger.fatal('Server could not process');
logger.debug("Some debug messages");
```

Run it again and you will get a new output response, shown in Figure 50.

Figure 49: Running application with log4js-node

Figure 50: Changing default value with own category name

By default, log4js-node writes the message on the console. If you want to write all messages in a file, you can configure a logging file. To get started:

1. Activate file logging by calling loadAppender()

2. Configure the file logging configuration and category name.

For instance, we store the log file on c:\temp\myapplication.log with the category name **myapplication**. Here is a code illustration:

```
var log4js = require('log4js');

log4js.loadAppender('file');
log4js.addAppender(log4js.appenders.file('c:\temp\myapplication.log'),
'myapplication');

var logger = log4js.getLogger('myapplication');
logger.info('Application is running');
logger.warn('Module cannot be loaded.');
logger.error('Saved data was error');
logger.fatal('Server could not process');
logger.debug("Some debug messages");
```

Run this code. Then, you will get a log file, myapplication.log. If you open it, you will see the file content as follows:

```
[2012-10-26 21:43:36.531] [INFO] myapplication - Application is running
[2012-10-26 21:43:36.546] [WARN] myapplication - Module cannot be loaded
[2012-10-26 21:43:36.547] [ERROR] myapplication - Saved data was error
[2012-10-26 21:43:36.547] [FATAL] myapplication - Server could not process
[2012-10-26 21:43:36.548] [DEBUG] myapplication - Some debug messages
```

For further information about log4js-node, visit https://github.com/nomiddlename/log4js-node.

Chapter 9 Events

Events enable an object to notify other objects when something of interest occurs. The object that sends (or raises) the event is called the publisher and the objects that receive (or handle) the event are called subscribers.

In this chapter, we're going to learn events implementation using Node.js.

Events Module

Node.js provides an **events** module to manipulate communication based on an event. For further information this module, you can visit the events module document on http://nodejs.org/api/events.html.

Getting Started

Let's start writing the event code. We use the EventEmitter object to create our events. Don't forget to load the events module.

First, we prepare a function as a callback function and pass it into the on() function from the EventEmitter object. Here is sample code if the caller sends an event message that is the same with on():

```
var EventEmitter = require('events').EventEmitter;
var myEmitter = new EventEmitter;


var connection = function(id){
    // do something
    console.log('client id: ' + id);
};
myEmitter.on('connection', connection);

myEmitter.on('message', function(msg){
    // do something
    console.log('message: ' + msg);
});
```

To test it, write this script:

```
myEmitter.emit('connection', 6);
myEmitter.emit('connection', 8);
myEmitter.emit('message', 'this is the first message');
myEmitter.emit('message', 'this is the second message');
myEmitter.emit('message', 'welcome to nodejs');
```

Explanation:

- First, we load the events module.

- Define the EventEmitter object and instantiate it.

- We can define a function variable or put the function into the on() method directly.

- To send the message, we can use the emit() method with the event name and data as parameters.

After writing the code, run it in the console. Here is program output of our application:

Figure 51: Executing an application with the events module

Once Event Listener

If you use the on() method, it means this event listener will listen for the event forever until the application closes. If you plan to listen for the event once, you can use the once() method.

Please write this sample code:

```
var EventEmitter = require('events').EventEmitter;

var myEmitter = new EventEmitter;

myEmitter.once('message', function(msg){
    // do something
    console.log('message: ' + msg);
});

myEmitter.emit('message', 'this is the first message');
myEmitter.emit('message', 'this is the second message');
myEmitter.emit('message', 'welcome to nodejs');
```

Try to run this code. The sample of program output can be seen in Figure 52.

Figure 52: A simple application for once event usage

You can see that once the event function receives one event, it will stop to listen for another event.

Remove Events

If you want to remove the event listener, call removeListener(). This function needs an event name and a function variable for parameters.

Here is a sample code for how to remove the 'connection' event.

```
var EventEmitter = require('events').EventEmitter;
var myEmitter = new EventEmitter;

// functions
var connection = function(id){
    // do something
    console.log('client id: ' + id);
};
var message = function(msg){
    // do something
    console.log('message: ' + msg);
};

// waiting event
myEmitter.on('connection', connection);
myEmitter.on('message', message);

// send message
myEmitter.emit('connection', 6);
// remove event
myEmitter.removeListener('connection',connection);

// test to send message
myEmitter.emit('connection', 10);
myEmitter.emit('message', 'welcome to nodejs');
```

Run it. You can see the program output in Figure 53.

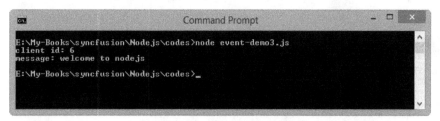

Figure 53: Removing event listener

Since the removeListener() function was called, the event didn't listen to the 'connection' event so the program only shows once.

Chapter 10 Web Applications

In this chapter, we're going to learn web programming similar to PHP but we'll implement it using Node.js. There are a lot of web frameworks for Node.js. For our scenario, we'll use a basic HTTP Node.js module and **Express.js**.

Getting Started

Node.js provides http modules to manipulate and handle the HTTP request and response. You can read this API on http://nodejs.org/api/http.html.

Let's write this code:

```
var http = require('http');


var server = http.createServer(function (req, res) {
    res.write('Welcome to http nodejs');
    res.end();

});

server.listen(8084);
console.log('Server is running on port 8084');
```

Save this code into a file, for instance, web-demo1.js.

Now we start to run this application:

```
node web-demo1.js
```

When executing this application for the Windows platform, you will get the form dialog shown in Figure 54. It's better to check **Private Network** and then click **Allow access**.

The sample of the program output can be seen in Figure 55. Now you can open a browser and write the URL:

```
http://localhost:8084/
```

Then you will get a response in the browser as shown in Figure 56.

Figure 54: Confirming from Windows Firewall to open a port

Figure 55: Executing a simple web application

Figure 56: Accessing a web application using a browser

To work with web applications:

- First, load the HTTP module.

- Create a web server by calling `createServer()`

- We get the request and response objects (`req, res`)

- Handle the request and response from the client using these objects.

- Call `end()` to close sending the response to the client.

- We call `listen()` with a port parameter, for example 8084, to activate the listening process.

To stop the application, press Ctrl+C.

Manipulating an HTTP Header

We can get header information from a client request and send a response with a custom header.

We can get header information from a client request from `req.headers` directly. We can also set a custom header attribute by calling `setHeader()` from the response object (`res`).

Here is sample code for manipulating an HTTP header:

```
var http = require('http');

var server = http.createServer(function (req, res) {
    // print request header
    console.log(req.headers);

    // set response header
    res.setHeader('AppId','123456');
    // send response
    res.write('Welcome to http nodejs');
    res.end();

});

server.listen(8084);
console.log('Server is running on port 8084');
```

Run this code and open the browser application. Send a request to the server, for instance http://localhost:8084/. Then look at your console application. You will get a program output as shown in Figure 57.

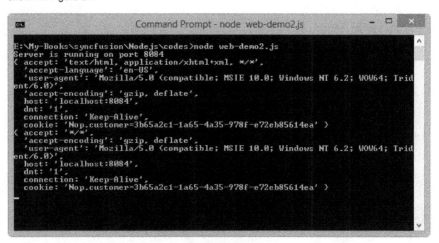

Figure 57: Printing information about HTTP request header

Handling Page Requests

In the previous section, we learned how to create simple web application. Now we'll continue to explore the HTTP module.

We can handle page requests from the client, for example:

- page /

- page /customer

- page /admin

To handle these page requests, we can check them through a request object and call the url attribute. If it matches with your expectations, then you can do something in your code.

```
if(req.url=='/'){
    res.write('Welcome to http nodejs');
    res.end();
}else{//some code here}
```

Let's write a complete simple application. Here is the sample code:

```
var http = require('http');


var server = http.createServer(function (req, res) {
    console.log(req.url);

    if(req.url=='/'){
        res.write('Welcome to http nodejs');
        res.end();
    }else
    if(req.url=='/customer'){
        res.write('Welcome to Customer page');
        res.end();
    }else
    if(req.url=='/admin'){
        res.write('Welcome to Admin page');
        res.end();
    }else
    {
        res.write('Page not found');
        res.end();
    }

});
```

```
server.listen(8084);
console.log('Server is running on port 8084');
```

Run this code and open browser application. Try to request the server, for example http://localhost:8084/customer/. We will get the response shown in Figure 58.

Figure 58: A page responding to Node.js

Working with HTTPS

In this section, we'll work with HTTPS for Node.js. First, we should have an SSL Certificate. You can buy it or create a self-signed certificate.

I would like to share how to create a self-signed certificate using **openssl**. Download openssl for your platform on http://www.openssl.org. For the Windows platform, you can download the setup file on http://slproweb.com/products/Win32OpenSSL.html.

After it is installed, try to open CMD and type the following:

```
openssl
```

You will get the prompt > in your console.

If you got a warning message as follows:

```
WARNING: can't open config file: c:/openssl/ssl/openssl.cnf
```

Then try to type this in your console:

```
set OPENSSL_CONF=C:\OpenSSL-Win32\bin\openssl.cfg
```

Change the path of the file **openssl.cfg**. You can put it on the Environment Variables in the Windows OS. You can see this in Figure 59.

Figure 59: Setting OPENSSL_CONF

First, we generate a private key with 1024 length and store it to a file called **myserver.key**. Open your console CMD and be sure you are running it as the administrator. Type this script:

```
openssl genrsa -des3 -out myserver.key 1024
```

If you still failed, you should run your CMD with administrator privileges. If successful, you will get a response as shown in Figure 60. Enter your pass phrase for the SSL key.

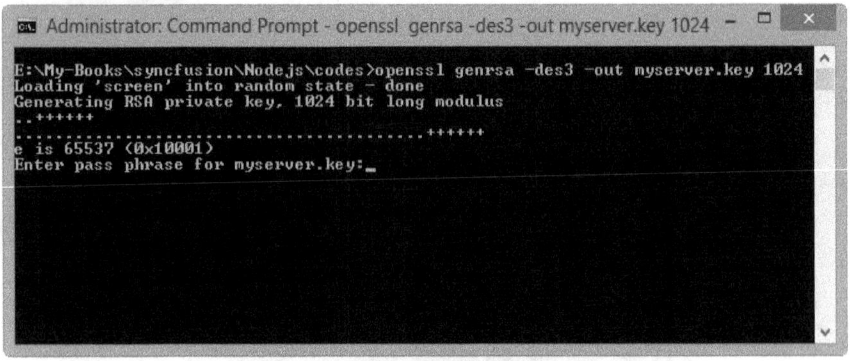

Figure 60: Creating an SSL key

Furthermore, we create a certificate file, called myserver.csr. Type this script:

```
openssl req -new -key myserver.key -out myserver.csr
```

Enter all fields. The sample response can be seen in Figure 61.

Now we need to sign our certificate. This means we are creating a self-signed certificate. Type the following commands:

```
openssl x509 -req -days 365 -in myserver.csr -signkey myserver.ke
y -out myserver.crt
```

Enter the pass phrase. You can see a sample of the console output in Figure 62.

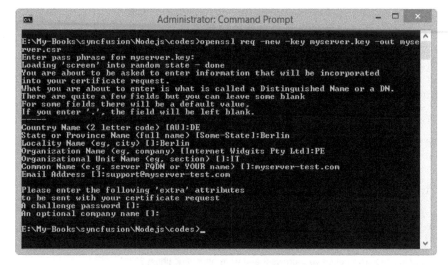

Figure 61: Creating a certificate file

Figure 62: Signing a certificate file

Now we can integrate our previous code (HTTP) with a certificate file to apply HTTPS.

Add certificate information on options objects such as key file, certificate file, and pass phrase. Here is the sample code:

```
var https = require('https');

var fs = require('fs');
var options = {
    key: fs.readFileSync('e:/ssl/myserver.key'),
    cert: fs.readFileSync('e:/ssl/myserver.crt'),
    passphrase: '1234'
};

var server = https.createServer(options,function (req, res) {
    res.write('Welcome to http nodejs');
    res.end();

});

server.listen(8084);
console.log('Server is running on port 8084');
```

Run this code. Then open your browser and write https://localhost:8084/.

Because we used a self-signed certificate, we get a warning message from our browser as shown in Figure 63.

Click **Continue to this website** and then you will get a response from the Node.js application, shown in Figure 64.

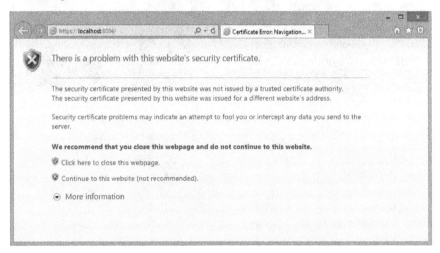

Figure 63: Warning message for self-signed certificate usage

Figure 64: Web application with HTTPS

Express.js

In the previous section, we used an HTTP module that is a part of the Node.js standard modules. We can use the Express.js library web framework. You get further information about Express.js from the official website, http://expressjs.com/. Here is a list of features:

- Robust routing

- Redirection helpers

- Dynamic view helpers

- Application level view options

- Content negotiation

- Application mounting

- Focus on high performance

- View rendering and partials support

- Environment-based configuration

- Session-based flash notifications

- Built on Connect middleware

- Executable for generating applications quickly

- High test coverage

These features could help you to accelerate web development and save development time.

Installation

The simple way to install Express.js is by using your **npm** manager. Before executing, your computer has already connected with the internet.

Type this command in your CMD:

```
npm install express
```

You also can install it globally.

```
npm install express -g
```

If it is successful, you will see the response as shown in Figure 65.

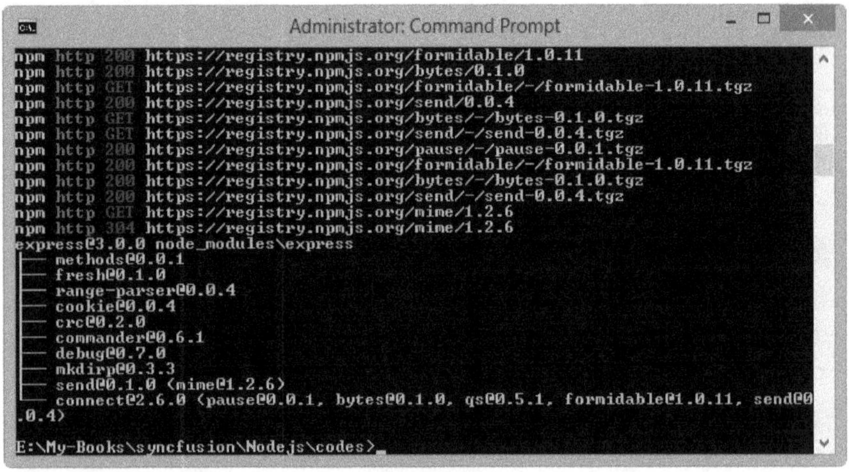

Figure 65: Installing Expressjs

Now we're ready to write code using Express.js.

Getting Started

We start to write a simple program using Express.js. We will create a web application.

Let's write this code:

```
var express = require('express');
var app = express();

app.get('/', function(req, res){
    res.send('Hello World Expressjs');
});

app.listen(8084);
console.log('Server is running on port 8084');
```

First, we include the Express.js module by calling require('express'). After that, we create the server object by instantiating the server object.

Furthermore, we create a response handler.

```
app.get('/', function(req, res){
    res.send('Hello World Expressjs');
});
```

At the end of code, we run a code listener on port 8084.

Now run it and open the browser. Write the URL http://localhost:8084/. You will get a response from the app as shown in Figure 66.

Figure 66: Getting a response from an Express.js app in browser

Handling Page Requests

To handle page requests in Express.js, you can call get() with the URL path as the parameter.

```
app.get('/', function(req, res){
    res.send('Hello World Expressjs');
});
```

We can add multiple request handlers in our code, for instance, '/customer' and '/admin' requests. You can write this sample code as follows:

```
var express = require('express');
var app = express();

app.get('/', function(req, res){
    res.send('Hello World Expressjs');
});
app.get('/customer', function(req, res){
    res.send('customer page');
});
app.get('/admin', function(req, res){
    res.send('admin page');
});

app.listen(8084);
console.log('Server is running on port 8084');
```

Run this code and open your browser by writing the URL http://localhost:8084/customer/. You will get a response from the customer page handling of the Node.js app, shown in Figure 67.

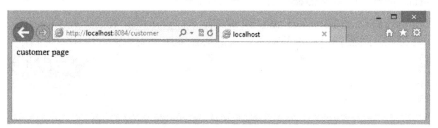

Figure 67: Response to /customer request from Expressjs app

Express.js with HTTPS

We can implement HTTPS in Express.js. It uses the HTTP Node.js standard module so you can handle it the same way as the HTTPS server.

```
var fs = require('fs');
var options = {
    key: fs.readFileSync('E:/ssl/myserver.key'),
    cert: fs.readFileSync('E:/ssl/myserver.crt'),
    passphrase: '1234'
};

var https = require('https');
var express = require('express');
var app = express();

app.get('/', function(req, res){
    res.send('Hello World Expressjs');
});

var server = https.createServer(options, app);
server.listen(8084);
console.log('Server is running on port 8084');
```

Run this code. You get the same response, shown in Figure 68.

Figure 68: Express.js app with HTTPS

Chapter 11 Socket Programming

A socket is one of the most fundamental technologies of computer networking. Sockets allow applications to communicate using standard mechanisms built into network hardware and operating systems. In this chapter, we will learn how to create a socket application using Node.js. Please note that the content in this chapter assumes you already know the basics of socket programming.

Socket Module

We can create an application based on the socket stack using a net module. You can find further information on net modules at http://nodejs.org/api/net.html.

Hello World

To get started, we create a simple application to get a list of IP addresses from the local machine. We can use the **os** module and call networkInterfaces() to get a list of network interfaces in our local machine. Each network interface provides information about an IP address.

Here is a code sample:

```
var os = require('os');

var interfaces = os.networkInterfaces();
for (item in interfaces) {
    console.log('Network interface name: ' + item);
    for (att in interfaces[item]) {
        var address = interfaces[item][att];

        console.log('Family: ' + address.family);
        console.log('IP Address: ' + address.address);
        console.log('Is Internal: ' + address.internal);
        console.log('');
    }
    console.log('==================================');
}
```

This code describes profiling for local networks. Run this code. The sample program output can be seen in Figure 69.

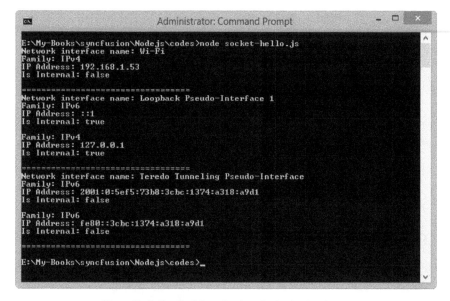

Figure 69: Getting the information from the local network

Client/Server Socket

The client/server model has become one of the central ideas of network computing. Most business applications being written today use the client/server model, including the TCP/IP network protocol.

Now we will create a client/server socket using Node.js. We will use a **net** module to build the client/server application. For our purposes, we will create a server socket and a client socket.

Server Socket

It is easy to create a server socket. The following is a simple algorithm on how to build a server socket:

1. Create the server socket.

2. Listen for the incoming client on the specific port.

3. If the client is connected, listen for incoming data and client disconnected events.

Now we can implement a server application using the socket with Node.js. Let's write this code:

```javascript
var serverPort = 9099;
var net = require('net');
var server = net.createServer(function(client) {
    console.log('client connected');
    console.log('client IP Address: ' + client.remoteAddress);
    console.log('is IPv6: ' + net.isIPv6(client.remoteAddress));
    console.log('total server connections: ' + server.connections);

    // Waiting for data from the client.
    client.on('data', function(data) {
        console.log('received data: ' + data.toString());

        // Write data to the client socket.
        client.write('hello from server');
    });

    // Closed socket event from the client.
    client.on('end', function() {
        console.log('client disconnected');
    });
});

server.on('error',function(err){
    console.log(err);
    server.close();
});

server.listen(serverPort, function() {
    console.log('server started on port ' + serverPort);
});
```

Save this code into a file called socket-server.js

Explanation

First, we create the server socket:

```javascript
var server = net.createServer(function(client) {

});
```

Inside the server socket, we're waiting for the incoming client socket. After the client is connected, we're waiting for the incoming message from the client using the on('data') event.

```
// Waiting for data from the client.
    client.on('data', function(data) {
        console.log('received data: ' + data.toString());

        // Write data to the client socket.
        client.write('hello from server');
    });

    // Closed socket event from the client.
    client.on('end', function() {
        console.log('client disconnected');
    });
```

We also try to catch errors that may occur.

```
server.on('error',function(err){
    console.log(err);
    server.close();
});
```

The server is running on port 9099.

```
var serverPort  = 9099;
var net = require('net');

server.listen(serverPort, function() {
    console.log('server started on port ' + serverPort);
});
```

Client Socket

A client socket is a client application that connects to the server and then sends and receives data from the server. We should know the IP address and port from the target server. We can call connect() to connect to the server. Use write() for sending data. To wait for incoming data from the server, we can use the data event.

The following sample code implements a client application:

```
var serverPort  = 9099;
var server = 'localhost';
var net = require('net');

console.log('connecting to server...');
var client = net.connect({server:server,port:serverPort},function(){
    console.log('client connected');

    // send data
    console.log('send data to server');
    client.write('greeting from client socket');
});

client.on('data', function(data) {
    console.log('received data: ' + data.toString());
    client.end();
});

client.on('error',function(err){
    console.log(err);
});
client.on('end', function() {
    console.log('client disconnected');
});
```

Save this code into a file called socket-client.js

The client app must know the server port and IP/hostname server.

After it is connected, the client app sends the data.

```
// Send the data.
console.log('send data to server');
client.write('greeting from client socket');
```

The client app also waits for the incoming message from the server and the occurred errors.
After it has received the server message, the client disconnects.

```
client.on('data', function(data) {
    console.log('received data: ' + data.toString());
    client.end();
});

client.on('error',function(err){
    console.log(err);
});
```

Testing

Now we can test our client/server application. First, we run the server application.

```
node socket-server.js
```

Then, execute the client application.

```
node socket-client.js
```

Here is the sample of program output for the server application:

Figure 70: Program output of server application

And the following is the program output for the client application:

Figure 71: Program output of client application

UDP Socket

We can create a client/server application with a UDP socket. This means we use connectionless-oriented communication. To implement the UDP socket, we will use the **dgram** module.

UDP Server

First, we call createSocket() to create the UDP socket from the **dgram** module. Pass the parameter **udp4** for the IPv4 environment or **udp6** for the IPv6 environment. After that, we start to listen for the incoming message using the message event and get a callback function with data and client object parameters. Don't forget to call bind() to bind to the listening port.

```
var dgram = require('dgram');
var server = dgram.createSocket('udp4');

var message = 'this server message';

server.on('message', function (data, client) {
    console.log('received data: ' + data);
    console.log('client ' + client.address + ':' + client.port);

});

server.on('listening', function () {
    var address = server.address();
    console.log('server listening on ' + address.address + ':' +
address.port);
});

server.bind(9094);
```

Save this code into a file called udp-server.js.

You can see that the server app waits for the incoming client connection.

```
server.on('listening', function () {
    var address = server.address();
    console.log('server listening on ' + address.address + ':' +
address.port);
});

server.bind(9094);
```

The server app also waits for the incoming message from the client.

```
server.on('message', function (data, client) {
    console.log('received data: ' + data);
    console.log('client ' + client.address + ':' + client.port);

});
```

UDP Client

You should create a UDP socket by calling createSocket() with the **udp4** or **udp6** parameter. To send a message to the UDP server, we can use the send() function with the message and server parameters.

```
var dgram = require('dgram');
var client = dgram.createSocket("udp4");

var server = 'localhost';
var serverPort = 9094;

// send message
var message = new Buffer("this is client message");
client.send(message, 0, message.length, serverPort, server, function(err,
bytes) {
    if(err)
        console.log(err);
    else
        client.close();
});
```

Save this code into a file called udp-client.js

As you can see in the code, the client app sends data and then closes the active connection.

```
client.send(message, 0, message.length, serverPort, server, function(err,
bytes) {
    if(err)
        console.log(err);
    else
        client.close();
});
```

Testing

First, we run the server application.

```
node udp-server.js
```

After that, execute the client application.

```
node udp-client.js
```

Here is sample of program output for the server application:

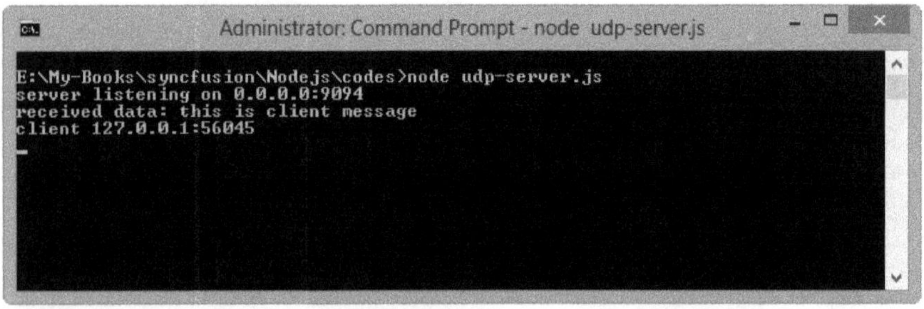

Figure 72: Program output for the UDP server

DNS

Domain Name System (DNS) is a database system that translates a computer's fully qualified domain name into an IP address. For further information about DNS modules, visit the Node.js documentation website, http://nodejs.org/api/all.html#all_dns.

We can use the **DNS** module to manipulate dns tasks, for example resolving the domain name. To resolve the domain name, we can call resolve4() for the IPv4 environment and resolve6() for the IPv6 environment. You can also use lookup() to resolve the domain name. It will return the IP address and family (IPv4 or IPv6).

Let's write the simple DNS app.

```
var dns = require('dns');

dns.resolve4('www.pecollege.net', function (err, addresses) {
    if (err)
        console.log(err);

    console.log('addresses: ' + JSON.stringify(addresses));
});

dns.lookup('www.pecollege.net', function (err, address, family) {
    if (err)
        console.log(err);

    console.log('addresses: ' + JSON.stringify(address));
    console.log('family: ' + JSON.stringify(family));
});
```

Save this code into a file called dns-demo.js. Run this code.

Figure 73: Simple app for DNS usage

Chapter 12 Socket.io

In this chapter, we will learn about one of the Node.js modules, Socket.io.

Getting Started

Socket.IO is a Node.js library. It aims to make real time apps possible in every browser and mobile device, blurring the differences between different transport mechanisms.

To install Socket.io, you can run the following script:

```
npm install socket.io
```

To get started, we must remember the Socket.io functions, especially emit() to send data to the Socket.io client and on('xxx') to listen for incoming data. Note that xxx is string-defined data.

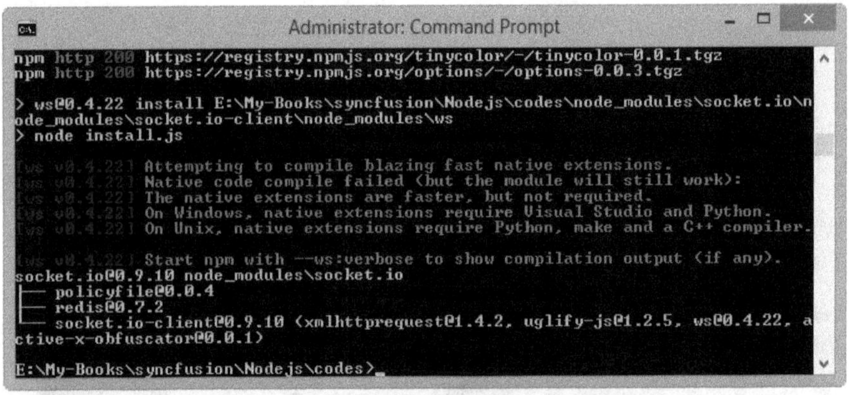

Figure 74: Installing Socket.io

Hello World

After you install the Socket.io module, we can start to create a Socket.io application.

Write the following script and save it as **socketio1.js**:

```
   var app = require('http').createServer(handler)
 , io = require('socket.io').listen(app)
 , fs = require('fs')

app.listen(8098);
console.log('server started on port 8098');
function handler (req, res) {
  fs.readFile(__dirname + '/index.html',
  function (err, data) {
    if (err) {
      res.writeHead(500);
      return res.end('Error loading index.html');
    }

    res.writeHead(200);
    res.end(data);
  });
}

io.sockets.on('connection', function (socket) {
  socket.emit('news', { content: 'news from server'});
  socket.on('feedback', function (data) {
    console.log(data);
    socket.emit('news', { content: 'news - ' + new Date() });
  });
});
```

To work with Socket.io:

1. Create the web server by calling `createServer()` with the handler function parameter.

```
   var app = require('http').createServer(handler)
```

2. The Socket.io object is passed into the http object.

```
 , io = require('socket.io').listen(app)
```

3. Activate listening on port 8098.

```
app.listen(8098);
```

4. In the handler function, we handle request/response to send the index.html file.

```
function handler (req, res) {
fs.readFile(__dirname + '/index.html',
function (err, data) {
  if (err) {
    res.writeHead(500);
    return res.end('Error loading index.html');
  }

  res.writeHead(200);
  res.end(data);
});
}
```

5. Wait for the incoming connection from the browser, the Socket.io client from index.html

```
io.sockets.on('connection', function (socket) {

});
```

6. Socket.io calls emit() to send data to the browser.

```
socket.emit('news', { content: 'news from server'});
```

7. Wait for the incoming data with the 'feedback' event and send data.

```
socket.on('feedback', function (data) {
  console.log(data);
  socket.emit('news', { content: 'news - ' + new Date() });
});
```

Next we create the **index.html** file and write the following script:

```
<html>
<head>
  <title>Demo Socket.IO </title>

<script src="/socket.io/socket.io.js"></script>
<script>
  var socket = io.connect();
  //socket.emit('feedback','this content from client');
  socket.on('news', function (data) {
    console.log(data);
    document.getElementById('newsContent').innerHTML = data.content;
    socket.emit('feedback', 'from client - ' + new Date());
  });
```

```
</script>

</head>
<body>
<span id='newsContent'></span>

</body>
</html>
```

Explanation

- First, we include Socket.io.js

- Instantiate the **socketio** object.

- Call on( ) to wait for the 'news' event from the server.

- If the client gets the data, **socketio** will send data to the server by calling emit()

To run the application, we must run the server file:

```
Node socketio2.js
```

Now open the browser and write the URL http://localhost/

Here is a sample program output for the server side:

Figure 75: Server side of Socket.io app

Here is a sample program output for the browser. Activate the browser console to see incoming data from the server.

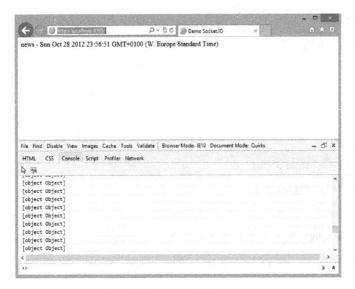

Figure 76: Browser as client app

Socket.io and Express.js

We can combine Sockect.io and Express.js. To illustrate this, we will use the same code from the previous section.

Write the following code and save as socketio2.js:

```
var express = require('express')
  , http = require('http');

var app = express();
var server = http.createServer(app);
var io = require('socket.io').listen(server);
console.log('server started');

app.get('/', function(req,res){
  res.sendfile(__dirname + '/index.html');
});

io.sockets.on('connection', function (socket) {
  socket.emit('news', { content: 'news from server'});
  socket.on('feedback', function (data) {
    console.log(data);
    socket.emit('news', { content: 'news - ' + new Date() });
  });
});

server.listen(8098);
```

Basically, we just pass the express object into the http object.

```
var express = require('express')
  , http = require('http');

var app = express();
var server = http.createServer(app);
var io = require('socket.io').listen(server);
```

Run this code and open the browser. You will get the same response from the application.

Real-Time Monitoring

Socket.io can be used to create a real-time application. The server can push data to the browser. The browser also can send data to the server.

To illustrate this, we will create real-time monitoring. In this scenario, the server pushes data to the browser. The browser will render graphics based on the data. Use the flot library (https://code.google.com/p/flot/) to visualize the data.

Download the flot library and extract it to your working folder.

Write the following code and save as socketio3.js:

```javascript
var http = require('http');
var net = require('net');
var path = require('path');
var fs = require('fs');

var port = 9088;

// Create an HTTP server.
var srv = http.createServer(function (req, res) {
        console.log('request starting...');

        var filePath = '.' + req.url;
        if (filePath == './')
                filePath = './realtime-demo.html';

        var extname = path.extname(filePath);
        var contentType = 'text/html';
        switch (extname) {
        case '.js':
                contentType = 'text/javascript';
                break;
        case '.css':
                contentType = 'text/css';
                break;
        }

        path.exists(filePath, function(exists) {

                if (exists) {
                        fs.readFile(filePath, function(error, content) {
                                if (error) {
                                        res.writeHead(500);
                                        res.end();
                                } else {
                                        res.writeHead(200, {
                                                'Content-Type' : contentType
                                        });
                                        res.end(content, 'utf-8');
                                }
                        });
                } else {
                        res.writeHead(404);
                        res.end();
                }
        });
```

```
});

gw_srv = require('socket.io').listen(srv);

srv.listen(port);
console.log('server started');
gw_srv.sockets.on('connection', function(socket) {
    var dataPusher = setInterval(function () {
        socket.volatile.emit('data', Math.random() * 100);
    }, 1000);


    socket.on('disconnect', function() {
        console.log('closing');
        //gw_srv.close();
        srv.close();
    });


}); // On connection
```

Now write the following realtime-demo.html:

```
<!DOCTYPE HTML PUBLIC "-//W3C//DTD HTML 4.01 Transitional//EN"
"http://www.w3.org/TR/html4/loose.dtd">
<html>
 <head>
    <meta http-equiv="Content-Type" content="text/html; charset=utf-8">
    <title>Flot Demo</title>
    <script language="javascript" type="text/javascript"
src="/flot/jquery.js"></script>
    <script language="javascript" type="text/javascript"
src="/flot/jquery.flot.js"></script>

    <script src="/socket.io/socket.io.js"></script>
    <script>
      var socket = io.connect();
      var items = [];
        var counter = 0;

      socket.on('data', function (data) {
          console.log(data);
          items.push([counter,data]);
          counter = counter + 1;
          $.plot($("#placeholder"), [items]);
      });
    </script>
```

```
    </head>
      <body>
      <h1>Flot Dmo</h1>
      <div id="placeholder" style="width:600px;height:300px;"></div>
      </body>
</html>
```

Run the following code:

```
node socketio3.js
```

Open the browser. You will get a response as shown in the following figure:

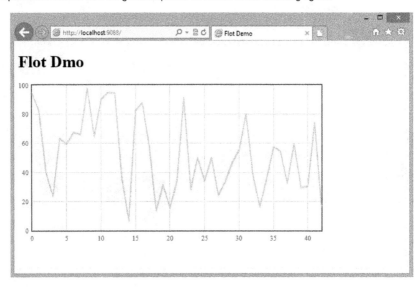

Figure 77: A simple app for visualizing the data

Chapter 13 Database Programming

A database consists of a collection of data such as text, files, audio, and video. Database programming may seem very complicated, but the reality is that it can be simple when you know the main steps. In this chapter, we're going to learn the basics of database programming.

Node.js Module for Database

Node.js can communicate with a database server through a database driver. We must install a database driver and the Node.js database module before we start to develop a database application.

Here is a list of Node.js database modules that we can use in our application:

* Microsoft SQL Server, https://github.com/joyent/node/wiki/Modules#wiki-db-mssql

* PostgreSQL, https://github.com/joyent/node/wiki/Modules#wiki-db-pg

* MySQL, https://github.com/joyent/node/wiki/Modules#wiki-db-mysql

* Sqlite, https://github.com/joyent/node/wiki/Modules#wiki-db-sqlite

* Oracle, https://github.com/joyent/node/wiki/Modules#wiki-db-oracle

* NoSQL, https://github.com/joyent/node/wiki/Modules#wiki-db-nosql

In this chapter, we will learn database programming for Sqlite, MySQL, and NoSQL (MongoDB database).

SQLite

In this section, we use the `node-sqlite3` module for node.js SQLite driver. You can get it on https://github.com/developmentseed/node-sqlite3 .

Execute the following script to install the SQLite driver for Node.js:

```
npm install sqlite3
```

I tried to install it on Windows but I got many problems due to SQLite library compatibility. The driver for SQLite is not only in JavaScript and hence requires Visual Studio to be installed in Windows. After installing Visual Studio a lot of tweaks need to be made. I recommend using the Linux or Mac platform for this scenario, or you may want to look for another SQLite for Node.js which supports the Windows platform. Another solution, you can compile node-sqlite3 from source code. Please read the installation document at https://github.com/mapbox/node-sqlite3#building-from-the-source .

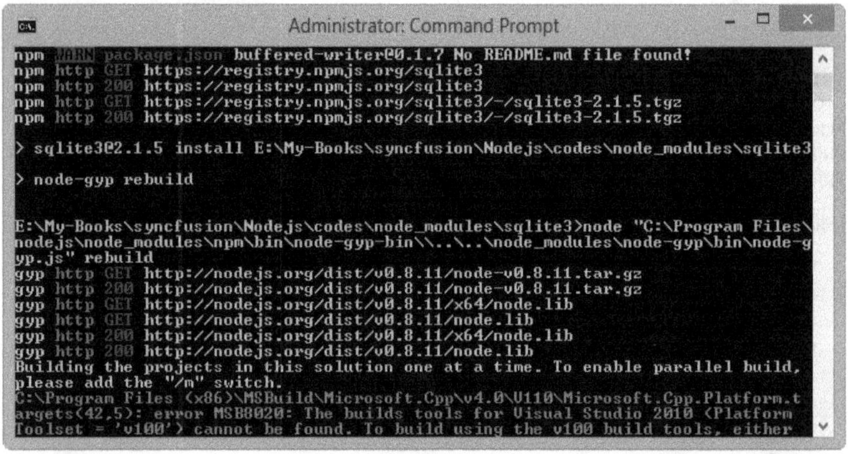

Figure 78: Installation problem for SQLite and Node.js on the Windows platform

For the Linux and Mac platforms, you must install the SQLite3 module via the npm manager as follows:

```
sudo npm install sqlite3
```

If you got an error, it may need required libraries as follows:

```
sudo apt-get install build-essential
sudo apt-get install sqlite3 libsqlite3-d
```

Now we can develop an application to access SQLite.

Here is the sample code for SQLite data manipulation, such as creating, inserting, and deleting:

```
var sqlite3 = require('sqlite3').verbose();
var db = new sqlite3.Database('mydatabase');

db.serialize(function(){
    // Create the table.
    db.run('CREATE TABLE customer(id NUMERIC,name TEXT)');

    // Insert the data.
    var query = db.prepare('INSERT INTO customer VALUES(?,?)');
    for(var i=0;i<5;i++){
        query.run(i+1,'customer ' + (i+1));
    }
    query.finalize();

    // Select the data.
    db.each('SELECT * FROM customer', function(err,row){
        if(!err){
            console.log(row.id + '----' + row.name);
        }else{
            console.log(err);
        }
    });
});

db.close();
```

MongoDB

To access MongoDB, we can use the node-mongodb-native module as the database driver.
You can get further information about this module at https://github.com/christkv/node-mongodb-native.

First, install MongoDB. If you have already installed it, skip these steps.

For the Ubuntu platform, update the repository:

```
sudo apt-key adv --keyserver keyserver.ubuntu.com --recv 7F0CEB10
sudo apt-get update
```

Install MongoDB and its driver for Node.js:

```
sudo apt-get install mongodb-10gen
sudo npm install mongodb
```

For the Mac and Windows platforms, you can download MongoDB and install it directly from the website, http://www.mongodb.org/.

To get started, we can create a simple app to connect to the MongoDB engine. Assume we have the MongoDB server in the local computer and database test.

We use the **mongodb** module and initiate the Server and **Db** objects. Call open() from the Db object to connect to the MongoDB server.

```
var mongo = require('mongodb'),
  Server = mongo.Server,
  Db = mongo.Db;

var server = new Server('localhost', 27017, {auto_reconnect: true});
var database = new Db('test', server);

database.open(function(err, db) {
  if(!err) {
    console.log("connected");
    // close connection
    db.close();
  }
});
```

The open() function gives a callback with the parameter error and database object. To close the database connection, call close().

We continue to create the application to insert data. First, we must open a collection (a table in the conventional database) that we want to use to insert data. Create the data, for example, employee with collection attributes, and call the insert() function to insert the data.

```javascript
var mongo = require('mongodb'),
  Server = mongo.Server,
  Db = mongo.Db;

var server = new Server('localhost', 27017, {auto_reconnect: true});
var database = new Db('test', server);

database.open(function(err, db) {
  if(!err) {
    console.log("connected");
    db.collection('employee',function(err,coll){
      var employee = {name:'user1',
                  email:'user1@email.com',
                  country: 'germany'};
    //Insert.
    coll.insert(employee,function (err){
        if(err)
          console.log(err);
        else
          console.log('inserted data was success');

        // Close connection.
        db.close();
    });

  });
  }
});
```